15 Minutes to a Better Interview

What I wish Every Job Candidate Knew

Russell Tuckerton

Introduction

Congratulations. You're about to hear direct "from the horse's mouth" how to interview better. Not from a recruiter, not from a human resources individual, but directly from a person who has made all hiring decisions for my staff over the last 20 years. Hiring managers make all final decisions. All other roles involved in the interview process are support roles. Not decision makers.

This book is about giving you a highly condensed summary of the most important things you need to know to not only interview well – but to have an advantage over other candidates.

I want to prevent you from making mistakes I've seen over the course of my hiring career that have caused qualified candidates **to not get the job offer**. It is meant to be immediately useful, and to reinforce the basics that will help you land your next job.

You should be able to review and internalize the key material in this book within 15 minutes.

This book is not a 300 page guide to interviewing. I think those are a waste of time. Often they are written by recruiters or human resources personnel who, quite honestly, have no say in whether someone is hired. They may control whether your resume gets to the hiring manager, but at the end of the day the hiring manager makes the decision. That's why you should listen to one. Reading through hundreds of questions and answers won't prepare you better. In fact, I would argue that will only confuse you and create a jumble of information you'll try to remember during the interview and end up getting flustered. Do you really want to read through 101 interview questions and try to remember how to respond to each one?

Interviewing well and getting the job offer isn't something that requires hours of learning. There are only a few critical things I consistently see candidates doing wrong, and if you understand those, you will fare better than other candidates who don't have this insight.

In my more than two decades of experience in the high tech industry, I've been a Director, Senior Director, and Vice President at several companies, ranging from Fortune 500 companies like Microsoft, to small startups. Crazy interviews are like bad auditions for a talent show, and I've experienced many!

What I Wish Every Job Candidate Knew

I've lost count of the number of times I really wanted to halt an interview and provide coaching to a job candidate. They look great on paper, and their actual work experience and education are a near perfect match for my organization. They perform well on the phone screening with human resources, and then they totally blow it when they interview with me in person.

The various chapters in this book go into greater depth about things you need to know about the interviewing process - how to prepare, how to answer key questions, and how to act during an interview. I have intentionally condensed all this into a form you can read, absorb, and begin using quickly – within 15 minutes in most cases. Learn the game, and you can dramatically raise your odds of getting almost any job.

For now I'm going to give you some very high level basics to incorporate into how you approach and conduct yourself during an interview. If you read nothing else in this book, read these.

Get the Basics Right

If you are interviewing for a job, you need to pay attention to just a few simple rules of thumb. Let these guide your answers and demeanor when interviewing:

- **Dress up.** I don't care what level or type of job you are interviewing for, always dress up, even if the office environment or position is casual dress. This shows respect for the company and the individuals interviewing you.

- **Whether this is your dream job or not, act as though it is.** I want people who are excited about my company, my group, and the work we are doing. If I am your second or third choice – hide it. Otherwise, I will pick up on your lack of interest and enthusiasm and your resume will be in the circular file before you leave the building.

- **Do not ramble.** Answers should be short and concise, unless asked to "tell a story" about your career or background. To a manager or executive, ramblers come across as unfocused, dancing around a question, and lacking an ability to focus on the key facts. Even if telling a story [my favorite is "tell me about your career"], keep it logical, at the right level, and wrap it up within 3-5 minutes at most. Hit the key points only.

- **Research my company and our products.** If you don't demonstrate some initiative ahead of coming in, why would I ever think you'd have any if you were hired? Learn enough to ask intelligent questions during the interview. More examples are provided later to stimulate your thinking.

- **This is about what you can do for my team and my company.** Don't focus on why the benefits are good for you, the location is close to your home, or you've heard it is a fun environment. Demonstrate why you want this position, and how your experience and education can deliver what we need done.

- **When providing examples, emphasize teamwork.** The role of individual contributor sitting in a cube all day is all but gone. Companies need people who work well with others and help the entire team win.

- **Provide alternate but related examples if you don't match a direct experience question.** Example – If you have project managed a large team but without direct reports, relate this experience, skills, challenges, etc. to how they make you a perfect fit as a new people manager.

- **Don't volunteer personal information**. I don't want to know if you have kids, a happy marriage, or car problems. Furthermore, this speaks to a lack of discipline in protecting what I consider private information, which can be deadly for some positions. You also don't want a hiring manager to begin worrying about your work schedule with respect to commute, child care, sick relatives, dogs, etc. Don't go there.

- **Be confident but not arrogant**. Whether any of us like it or not, a strong confident approach will always win over a meek, nervous one. Pay attention to body language – do some research into this area, if needed, beyond what I present here.

- **Always ask about next steps**. Do not ask if you seem to be a fit, or if you are missing any skills they deem necessary. This comes across as insecurity, and I've never hired anyone who wanted a readout at the end of the interview on how it went and what his or her strengths were. I am amazed at the number of people who never ask about next steps – as if this isn't important to them.

- **Your interview starts when you get out of your car/train/bus**. Do you know many companies include the shuttle driver, the front desk receptionist, the "office tour guide", and many others as part of the interview team? Treat every single person you meet with respect and enthusiasm for the company. You don't know where the hidden assessment is occurring.

- **You want the job for the challenges and ability to make contributions based on your skills and experience**. Never come across as just wanting any job, or needing benefits, or stability, etc. I want people who want the role in my group for the right reasons.

5

Responding to Questions

Expanding upon the basics you just read, responding to questions during an interview can be summarized into the following three areas:

- How you respond
- What you respond with
- Your body language

How You Respond

"How you respond" refers to the pause between the question and your response, the tone of your voice, the length of the response, and how concise the answer was. Always pause after a question and look thoughtful [2-4 seconds is good, depending on the complexity of the question]. Candidates who reply too quickly come across as not thinking about the question or not taking it seriously, and mentally I am already set to hear a canned or unrelated response. Don't underestimate the damage an "immediate response" can do. Use your judgment, based on the complexity of the question, but always "think" about your response before letting your mouth start moving.

Your tone of voice should reflect the material you are responding with, but should never be monotone. You should show excitement, be contrite when appropriate, and be serious or light hearted, depending on the subject of your response. Be human.

The length of the response, of course, varies with the question asked. In general, most of my questions are intended to elicit a 3-4 sentence response or less – but one that is highly focused on what I asked. Some questions are "story" questions, and these may take 3-5 minutes to answer. As an example, I almost always ask candidates to describe their careers to me, as I want to see how they sum up their experiences in their own words as well as any emotional or body language cues tied to their experiences.

A near perfect response to that particular story question typically starts with early education, training, etc. and then walks me through each subsequent job – but only spending 3-4 sentences on each job, including the role performed, growth achieved, and reason for moving to the next one. Do not ramble, and do not surface irrelevant facts (I've had candidates go on for minutes about how good the cafeteria was and the benefits at a previous position – not good).

What You Respond With

Interview questions are designed to help the hiring manager understand you better as a person as well as whether you are qualified and can be successful in the role. Specifically, responses to questions are evaluated across many of the following categories (note that not all of these will apply to all roles):

- Do you have the education/training that is relevant to what this role requires? If not, can you demonstrate you can learn quickly and be effective? (What examples are provided to illustrate this?)

- Are you a team player, or more interested in personal credit and recognition? Will you work well with others? Do you help others even if "not part of your job description"?

- Are you mature? Do you get emotional or have unprofessional reactions to tough situations?

- Do you learn from past mistakes? I've never hired someone who couldn't provide a past mistake and what they learned from it.

- Will you fit in with the team? Will people respect you?

- Do you have critical thinking skills? Can you recognize what is important and not important in a given situation and not get bogged down in details?

- Do you communicate well both verbally and non-verbally? Are you concise, respectful, and able to provide the relevant information in any given situation?

- Can you manage conflict – whether with co-workers, managers, or subordinates?

- Do you put the interests of the company first?

- Are you a "go getter", or will you be a wall flower? I seldom am interested in hiring wallflowers.

Some other key items include never "bad mouthing" your previous boss, company, or co-workers. Always position conflict or reasons for leaving a company in a positive, educational light that made you a stronger person or reflected a change in career path.

One warning sign to watch out for: if a hiring manager asks you the same question, slightly rephrased, twice, then this is a sign you aren't providing the information needed from the question asked. Treat this as a WARNING. It means you need to stop and think a little more about the question and consider why the question is being asked relative to the categories outlined above, and then tailor your response to this.

To be honest, if I have to ask more than 3 or 4 questions over again because of poor responses, this is usually enough for me to terminate the interview, as my decision has already been made not to hire.

Conversely, if more than 2 or 3 responses are too lengthy, ramble and meander all over the place, I'm usually done with that candidate as well.

Remember – concise, relevant answers that don't have any personal, judgmental, or negative connotations in them.

Here are some great general questions to pick from to ask during the interview – **always** augment these with specific questions based on your research of the company and its products/services:

- What are the key challenges you see for this position?

- What are the priorities for the next 3 months for this role? What will success look like at that time?

- Is this a new role in the organization? If so, can you tell me more about the growth that resulted in the need for the role?

- What are the 3 top attributes or skills you think are needed to be successful in this role?

- What brought you to this company – e.g. what excites you about the company and the direction it is headed?

- How would you describe the culture of the company/group/etc.?

- What is your management style?

Body Language

Entire books have been written about this topic. Don't read them. You only need to know a few basics (practice these in different settings so you get used to them without having to think about it):

- Don't slouch. Sit up straight - legs crossed is fine - and monitor your hands. Hands should be visible and in a natural position on your legs, crossed, etc. Under no circumstances should you cross your arms on your chest [negative body language], sit on your hands, or otherwise have them hidden in pockets, etc.

- Sporadically lean in to the conversation. This indicates interest and excitement about what is being discussed.

- Talk with your hands if this is normal for you. Again this shows interest and engagement in the topic being discussed.

- For "big" or "important" questions, don't feel afraid to lean forward with your hands on the table in front of you when you give your response. Use this sparingly, but it is very effective when responding with critical information.

- Don't play with your lips, ears, clothes, etc. Your hands shouldn't be viewed as some rogue agents that slipped into the interview.

- Always make eye contact. However, there is an entire field of study around mimicking the person you are talking to. Without going too deeply into this field of study, if the person interviewing you frequently breaks eye contact, then you should mirror them when you are responding or listening to them. If they are always looking into your eyes, then you should do the same. The theory is people like people like themselves, and if someone has body language similar to theirs, it makes them feel more comfortable subconsciously.

- No heavy perfumes, cologne, or a ton of jewelry. Keep it tasteful.

- Always greet an interviewer with a handshake and eye contact, and always exit the interview with a handshake and eye contact (and thanking them for their time and the opportunity to be part of the company).

Later in this book is a set of 7 very important interview questions. These questions cover most categories you may be asked and provide real world responses I've received, along with explanations of why they were good or bad, and most importantly why the question was asked and what response is expected. If you understand the material around these 7 questions, you will find yourself prepared to answer almost any question with a great answer, and avoid traps and pitfalls others have fallen into.

Questions Not to Ask

This section is short and sweet. However, about every 4th candidate I interview will ask one or more of these questions, and seldom are they the top candidates I hire. Please do not ask these in an interview.

<u>Off Limits:</u>

Any family-related or personal questions, regardless of whether pictures are on the desk or not showing I have a family.

Any question around benefits, salary, pay increases, bonuses, perks of the office, flex time, etc.

Any question around work hours unless there are fixed shifts for this role and therefore would be relevant to whether the position is a good fit for you.

Any question around working from home, vacation, days off, etc.

Avoid any special circumstances you may need around periodic school functions, community work you may do, etc. Unless it is something that will impact your ability to work core hours every day, wait until you get the job offer to negotiate this. At the point of the job offer the company wants you; they've made their decision and will be much more inclined to consider special circumstances to get you on board.

Aligning Your Experience With The Position

It is rare that a position you are applying for exactly matches your past jobs. What hiring managers are looking for is how well past jobs have prepared you to do what this new role requires – what have you learned and how well do you generalize that experience to different positions.

Don't dismiss school projects or unrelated work experience where you can demonstrate teamwork or initiative, and even volunteer work such as at a school, a shelter, food bank, etc. Being able to demonstrate your work ethic and approach to the needs of a job across seemingly unrelated experiences will differentiate you as a candidate.

Entry Level Position Example

You're applying for a phone technical support position for a software product. I would want to know if you have:

- Any past experience with this product or similar products (Be sure you researched this ahead of time).

- Knowledge of the subject matter the software covers – e.g. accounting, entertainment, utilities, etc.

- Good personal communication skills (How will you sound to my customers on the other end of the phone?).

- Experience in a customer service position, whether it be retail or working a bake sale – anything showing you understand how to interact with customers directly. I want to see some initiative here.

- The ability to learn fast and find answers for customers, even if you don't know them yourself.

- Coachability – I'd love to see an example from school or previous jobs where you were coached by a manager and learned how to excel at something. After all, I will be teaching you how we perform technical support at my company and want you to be like a sponge.

The goal is to find aspects of almost any past experience that play into the skills that are important in this job. Have you helped others with their computer problems? Are you good at repairing your bicycle? Do you like to take things apart and put them together again? Were you a team lead on a school project? Hopefully you see the trend here: You can find almost any experience that has aspects that are relevant.

Team Lead or Management Position Example

What I am looking for here is the ability to take senior management objectives and translate them into tasks and objectives for a team to accomplish. This includes inspiring them to perform their best, setting up mechanisms to assign, train, monitor, and complete the work, and manage and coach the people reporting to you.

I'm not just interested in past management experience. I've known too many bad managers who have been doing it for years. Often a team lead position is an individual's first foray into a people management position, so past management experience isn't as relevant.

Here are items you need to pull from your past work experience (and school or community work if applicable):

- Examples of how people looked up to you, or naturally came to you for guidance or advice.

- How you handle conflict among teams constructively.

- How you've held people accountable for getting something done.

- Examples of tough conversations about performance, attitude, etc. - even with peers.

- Sports or academic/hobby leadership: Were you in any kind of lead role, or if not, what did you most respect and learn from coaches?

- Anecdotes that show you to be approachable and have good communication skills.

- Evidence that you can take somewhat complicated tasks and break them down into activities a team needs to execute on.

- Examples that show you can be firm, yet approachable and "human".

One key and very difficult task of a people manager is holding people accountable for the work they need to perform - coaching under-performers, spreading skills from your top performers to others, and, when needed, being able to let people go, whether due to performance issues or layoffs. Showing confidence and willpower speaks to your ability to do this even without past experience.

Senior Management Position (e.g. Senior Manager, Director)

If you are ready for this level, or have been at this level for a while, then what I say below should resonate strongly. Being able to draw parallels and real examples from your past history, both as an individual contributor and as a manager, across the following areas is key:

- Ability to think strategically, and to align company objectives with the work your team needs to perform. This will require a demonstrated business acumen, often around financial, marketing, product, and competitive areas. This acumen will allow you to translate the strategy into lower level objectives to deploy to your team.

- Ability to drive change. More important than ever, companies need to be nimble and be able to change direction quickly. Highlight changes you have driven into your teams in the past – whether they cover people's skills, processes, or culture. Be sure and speak to the business outcome of these changes.

- Ability to digest company and team strategy and direction, and question it where appropriate, both for clarification, and to drive others to think outside the box. Most hiring managers are not just looking for "yes" people. We want leaders who bring their intellect and experiences to the table to make our company better.

- Ability to form and nurture relationships. Work gets done across companies not just by decree, but because people know and trust you and your intentions. Help others meet their needs, and you will find they will help you when you need it. Reaching this level and moving even higher is more based on relationships and politics than on your individual skills or accomplishments.

- Ability to learn from mistakes, both with your direct reports and with your peers/superiors. I personally always ask about a past mistake or error in judgment made, and am intent on seeing what you learned from it and how it influenced your future behavior.

- Ability to recognize good and bad cultures and know how to influence and slowly change the culture of a team. Throwing a bunch of bright people together doesn't mean they will accomplish great things. The culture of an organization led by a Sr. Manager or Director is key to the team performing at their highest level.

- Ability to take responsibility. I want to know you can hold yourself accountable for your team's performance, and examples of this both good and bad ("challenges") really speak to your leadership style.

- Ability to describe your leadership style. The stock answer here often revolves around not micro-managing, enabling your team with the skills and resources they need, etc, and creating a team-oriented culture where rewards and recognition focus on the accomplishments of the team over the individual.

Think about your past roles in light of the above, and have examples in the back of your head that demonstrate that you can operate at this level and in this environment. Questions will cover most, if not all, of the areas above, so doing a little prep work relative to your past experience in these areas will pay dividends during your interview.

7 Key Interview Questions

What is important when reading this chapter is to understand why the question is being asked (e.g. What am I or other hiring managers really looking for), and extrapolate the examples of good and bad answers to understand why they are good or bad. The good answers aren't meant to be used completely verbatim for every job interview you have; they are meant to provide a broad-based category of what a good response covers. You should then **tailor** the intent of the good response to the specific company, position, and role you are pursuing.

Question #1: Why are you interested in this position / our company?

Purpose: Determine if a candidate is here for the right reasons. This will speak to his (or her) interest in the company, products and services provided, and why he thinks he would be a good fit.

Good Responses

- I think the direction your company is headed with <XYZ> is very innovative and positioning you as a leader in the market, and I am excited about the opportunity to apply my skills and experience to contribute to this growth and innovation, while continuing my professional development in a world class organization.

- This position represents several unique challenges, and I am excited about applying my skills and background to tackle these challenges from both a company contribution as well as a personal growth perspective. I take customer service very seriously and feel it is critical to the success of both the company and your customers, and welcome the opportunity to work with your customers to ensure they have a great experience with these products.

- This role is perfectly aligned with where I want to grow my career and what I've been working towards, and given my skills and experiences, I feel I can make a significant contribution to both this team and company, and, as part of the overall team, help drive the company to the next level.

Bad Responses

- The company or office is close to my home and it would be a convenient commute for me.

- My friend works here and said it is a lot of fun.

- Your company is ranked one of the best places to work, and I've heard it has great benefits which is important to me.

Note that even a good response can transition into a bad response if it is expanded upon too much, or if the response wonders away from the original intent of the question. While the above are fairly obvious bad answers, keep in mind that good responses should be kept concise and very focused on the role and the question asked.

Positioning possible negatives from your past

This category doesn't really apply to this question. However, always be passionate about your interest in both the company and the position you are interviewing for. Don't focus on how good the company is for employees in terms of ranking, reputation, etc., or - most importantly - why it is good for you [location, salary, benefits, etc]. What we want to hear is a genuine passion and interest in the type of work you are interviewing for, and knowledge of the company's products and services <u>and why these excite you</u>.

Question #2: Why are looking to leave your current position?

Purpose: Determine why an employee possibly isn't happy or satisfied with their current or past position, and if these reasons would result in their not being happy or productive in the new position.

Good Responses

- My previous role was very rewarding and enabled me to make a contribution to the company and its customers; however, I feel I am ready to take on a larger role and set of responsibilities, and my current company is not at a stage where they can offer me this opportunity.

- I've really enjoyed doing <XYZ> for that company, and am ready to take that experience and my skill set and move into a new role at a growing company to continue on my career path. My current [previous] company understands this but simply can't offer me that type of opportunity right now.

- The company has recently changed its business strategy, which has resulted in less investment and emphasis in this area of the business, and consequently I don't feel as challenged as I once was. At this stage in my career I want to continue growing my skills and abilities in a challenging and growth-oriented business.

Bad Responses

- I'm not happy with the pay or benefits; I was passed over for a promotion.

- I don't get along with my manager; my manager doesn't like me; I can't get along with my coworkers.

- The commute is too long; the work hours don't fit my schedule; they require too much overtime.

Positioning possible negatives from your past

If you were laid off from your previous role

My company went through a reorganization due to a change in strategy or to reduce costs, and my position was eliminated as a result.

If you were terminated (fired)

- I made an error in judgment in how I expressed my disagreement with the direction the company was taking and they let me go as a result. It was a great learning experience for me in terms of how to constructively provide input without alienating myself from the management team, and I would certainly handle it differently in hindsight.

- I took on a set of responsibilities that, in hindsight, I was not prepared to handle and deliver on. It was a great learning experience and taught me to be very honest with myself and others when considering future roles and responsibilities, and to have a realistic assessment as to what role I am right for and which ones are not a fit for me.

- I didn't handle a personnel conflict with a colleague well, and while it resulted in the company and me parting ways, it taught me several valuable lessons around constructive and positive ways to resolve conflicts with colleagues. If I could go back and do it over again I'm confident I would approach the situation much more constructively and result in a win-win for myself, my colleagues, and the company.

If you have a long gap between your last role/position

Note: Use the most appropriate response based on your personal situation, and tailor the context appropriately.

- After being let go from my previous company, I took some time off to reflect on what is important to me in my career, and to ensure I had time to update my skills and perspective ahead of moving into my next role.

- It was important to me to ensure our children had a parent at home to ensure we established a solid foundation for their growth and development; now that they are <XYZ> I am ready to re-enter the work force and contribute my skills and experience to the success of your company.

- **AVOID:** I've been interviewing for the last <XYZ> months / looking for a position.
  *Managers are very sensitive to someone that has been unemployed for a long duration AND has been interviewing that entire time – if other companies did not want to hire you, it makes us wonder why and tends to influence us **to not be the ones to take a risk** where others weren't willing. A much better answer is taking time off to travel, for family, to recharge and refresh your skills, etc.*

Question #3: What is important to you in a work environment?

Purpose: To understand what candidates focus on when they are in roles at a company. Are they focused on the right behaviors and cultural environment.

Good Responses

- I like to be surrounded by colleagues who are intelligent, and very passionate and energized about what they do. This fuels my energy levels and helps me perform at my peak.

- I like an atmosphere of teamwork. Success comes not from celebrating my individual successes, but from feeling that I made a contribution to the team. Companies that celebrate team successes motivate individuals like me always to give their best back to the company.

- I love to be in an environment where I know I am helping make a company's customers successful. Providing exceptional customer service and seeing the impact I can have on each customer really motivates me and continues to build the reputation of the company as one that values their customers and is helping them be successful.

Bad Responses

- I like to have a large desk and personal work space and not sit too close to people.

- Good benefits, amenities like cafeteria and gym, and flexible work hours.

- An environment that provides good career opportunities as I want to move up in the organization fast *(Note: Managers think, "You haven't even got this job and you're already after the next position – denied!")*

Positioning possible negatives from your past

You're unlikely to have past experiences that would surface during this question. However, always avoid any physical aspects of a work environment when answering this question [amenities, commute time, benefits, etc.]. We are looking for the cultural aspects of a company that motivate you to success and contribute your best to the organization. If the most important work environment item is having an onsite gym, you aren't the right fit for our company.

Question #4: Why should we hire you / What makes you the best candidate for this role?

Purpose: Assess the candidates self confidence in their ability to meet and exceed the responsibilities of this position. If candidates aren't confident in their abilities, this can cause performance issues later down the line if hired.

Good Responses

- While many candidates will bring similar skills to this role, my passion for this type of position and personal drive for success will allow me to apply these skills to meet and exceed the responsibilities of this role.

- The combination of my skills, experience, and exceptional team-oriented approach, as demonstrated in my previous roles, is a combination that is hard to duplicate, and will produce results in this role for your company. My experience at <XYZ> is directly applicable to the business results needed in this role and demonstrates the level of contribution I can make as part of a strong team.

- Having the right skills is not enough to ensure success; my experience working in a variety of roles and across entire organizations *[Note: add in relevant experiences as appropriate]* has provided me with a strong ability to apply my skills to your team and contribute to the success of the team and the company.

Bad Responses

- was at the top of my class; I have my college degree; I'm smarter than others. *[Note: We don't want to hire someone who assumes he is smarter than everyone else. Large egos are a constant source of performance issues in any company.]*

- I'm a hard worker. *[Note: Everyone will be a hard worker. Why would we hire someone who isn't?]*.

- I get along well with everybody and would be fun to be around.

Positioning possible negatives from your past

You're unlikely to have past experiences that would surface during this question. However, always try and tie 1 or 2 specific experiences in your past [school or work experience] to the specific responsibilities of this position and/or the market this company is in. Remember – we've all gone to similar schools and learned similar skills. It is the application of those skills and the ability to be successful in a company culture that makes the difference.

Question #5: Tell me about a specific situation where you failed.

Purpose: People learn more from failures than successes. A candidate that has never "failed" at something has not taken any risks, which means he or she may not be right for us. This is a particularly tough question, as you have to mention a specific project, task, etc. that you weren't successful on, and people don't like to talk about their failures. We also want to see that you "learned" from a failure.

Good Responses

Note: the response to this question should be longer – you should spend 4-5 minutes responding to this question, and be sure to think for 30-60 seconds before answering. The short answers below are meant to provide guidance on how to communicate your longer experience and lessons learned. Substitute a specific task or responsibility below in place of the generic "task" based on your experiences.

- On Project XYZ we missed a critical deadline that delayed the delivery of the service. We missed this deadline because I had not obtained the buy-in of a key stakeholder in the project, and assumed he would simply be "on-board" with our approach. A key lesson I learned and have been using since then is to always clearly identify key stakeholders up front and spend time obtaining their buy-in and active support of the project's objectives and approach.

- A team member wasn't contributing his full effort to the job at hand. As a result, we didn't finish what we needed to do, and it not only hurt the company but reflected poorly on my performance. What I learned is that I should have pulled my co-worker aside and tried to understand why he wasn't motivated to deliver on his specific task. Was he too overwhelmed with other duties? Did he not understand what the task was and why it was needed? Or did he not have a perspective of the big picture, and how his efforts were critical to its success? I applied these questions to future situations and found that often it was one of these issues that was causing people not to be fully motivated to perform, and once we talked, they were energized about the task and delivered spectacular results. Going to the manager wouldn't have been as effective, and would have demonstrated a lack of ability on my part to get my team members to perform.

- When I was asked to do a task, I thought I knew what my manager wanted and simply took an approach based on this understanding, which ended up being wrong, and as a result my manager and colleagues had to do extra work to correct what I had already done. I learned to never assume that my understanding of a task was perfect, and to ask questions up front to clarify exactly what my manager needed, and to confirm my approach was the correct one to ensure that I delivered on exactly what was required.

Bad Responses

- I was late to work one day and missed completing a critical task that day, and my manager had no respect for my personal situation.

- I can't remember a time when something didn't go well, so I guess I don't really have a response to this question *[Note: This is one of the worst responses you can give as it indicates you're not honest about yourself and your experiences, and could paint you as an egomaniac].*

- I got written up because my attitude was horrible on a particular job, and it wasn't something I wanted to do anyway, nor did I consider it part of my job.

Positioning possible negatives from your past

This question is all about a negative experience in your past! However, you have to select an experience where you can demonstrate that you took a calculated risk and failed, but learned from this experience and were more successful in your next role/task/project.

It is important to always select something that, even if beyond your control, demonstrates how you changed your behavior in the future to accommodate for it. Nobody is perfect; no task or project is ever risk free, and people are expected to make mistakes. However, it shows introspection and a desire to learn and improve when you can communicate what you learned. that is what we are looking for.

We want people who aren't afraid to always be pushing their abilities to the next level, but recognize when they could have done something better and adopted this lesson on the next task they work on.

Question #6: Tell me about a past accomplishment you are especially proud of.

Purpose: This is where we want to hear about something you feel proud of. It can be from school, your personal life, or your past work experience. All are equally as valuable in helping us see what you consider important in your life.

Good Responses

As with the previous question, this response should take a bit longer, but not as long as the failure question. 3-4 minutes is typically a good response length, although going a bit longer is more preferable to a short answer. The responses below are meant to provide some examples of the type of successes you may want to highlight from your past and expand upon. A key item to include in every response at the end is to highlight what makes this one of your proudest accomplishments. Remember, these can be personal accomplishments such as "tutoring my son to take him from failing high school to graduating in the top of his class". A good answer need not always be found in work experience.

- I was the lead on a project we did for my college English class where we had to develop a complete play in 6 weeks. I loved working with my team – the energy and passion around our topic for the play was unbelievable, and the team just seemed to "click". We ended up winning the competition at the end of the semester, and I couldn't believe how good it felt to see so many people come together to accomplish something that looked impossible at first!

- We had an unusually large number of customers the day before Christmas that we had to service, and we were short staffed due to 3 colleagues being out sick. Although the temptation was there to stress out about the amount of work we had to do and complain about it, instead my colleague and I pulled everyone together for 5 minutes and positioned the upcoming work as a challenge. We put ourselves in the place of our customers, who through no fault of their own were going to have to wait longer to get serviced and likely be grumpy as a result, and decided to do everything we could to make this the best experience possible for our customers! By focusing on wanting them to have a good experience, we all felt a personal challenge that we wanted to see if we could deliver on. This was now a competition to see if we could individually and as a team work as we never had before and have fun doing it. This one 5 minute meeting and shift in perspective from "a long day at the job" to "Are we up for it? Are we strong enough to take on this challenge and help these customers have a better day?" resulted in our delivering record results that day – short staffed – and at the end of the day we celebrated our success!

- I had a customer on the phone who had been sold the wrong service about 6 months earlier from our company. She had valiantly tried to make it work, but was simply in the wrong package for what she wanted. She had called in almost in tears, and didn't have a lot of money to continue using the service and was just very upset and felt like it was her short comings and lack of intelligence that caused the service not to work all of these months. I really felt empathy for her, and wanted her to have a good experience with our company as I believe strongly in the services we offer. I put her on hold and spoke to my supervisor and asked her what we could to make the situation right. We jointly arrived at a full refund of the last 6 months of service, and a free month in another service package that would better meet her needs. I couldn't believe the gratitude my customer felt. She was in tears at this point and couldn't stop thanking me. This is a customer I will carry with me the rest of my life.

Bad Responses

Note: "Bad responses" to this question are generally superficial events from a candidate's past that don't illustrate any pride or passion in what was done. Too often candidates don't give this question a lot of thought and provide something that doesn't represent going above and beyond, or illustrating empathy, or a targeted focus. Everyday events that are considered part of your job, school, or "normal" life will never come across as a significant accomplishment and cause us to question your judgment as to what "accomplishment" means.

- I won a sales contest one week at work by being super aggressive with pushing our top packages to every customer.

- I had perfect attendance at work for 3 weeks in a row.

- I covered for a coworker one day when they called in sick to go to a concert.

Positioning possible negatives from your past

This question shouldn't be influenced by any potential negative past incidents – this is all about celebrating a big accomplishment and demonstrating the effort and passion you put into it.

Question #7: Tell me how you handle conflict at work.

Purpose: Conflict is unavoidable in a work place [or in life in general]. However, there are constructive ways to manage conflict, and destructive ways. Your response to this question will show us whether you can deal with the everyday situations that come up in a work place, or if your approach and way of dealing with these would be negative.

Good Responses

Your response to this question should reflect that you're aware that conflict naturally occurs – due to misunderstood objectives, steps to perform a job, personality conflicts, an irate or irrational customer, or someone simply having a bad day [maybe even yourself!]. A good response shows that you work to defuse the situation and then contribute to resolving it. Staying calm is always the first response, and sometimes it is acceptable to remove yourself from the situation temporarily to avoid its escalating, and then return to work to resolve the root cause. Communication and understanding other perspectives is always the key to resolving conflict, and this should be reflected in your answer when interviewing.

- In our weekly team meeting our supervisor presented a new sales commission plan that I and many others thought was unfair, and didn't reward our efforts in matching customers with our products. However, rather than react negatively and emotionally as some of my colleagues did, I scheduled a meeting with my supervisor later that day and asked him to explain the plan in more detail. It turns out there were excellent reasons for the change from a company and customer perspective, and there was actually a chance to make more money under the new plan for top performers. Had I reacted negatively in a group setting without getting more information, I would have damaged my career and my reputation with my peers and management team.

- A new administrative assistant started one week, and almost immediately she started treating me differently than other department members – ignoring my greetings, looking past me or not responding to my requests for assistance, and in general just being very negative towards me. She treated everyone else completely differently. It was reaching the point of being very uncomfortable even going into work and having to be around her. I finally one day asked her to have a cup of coffee with me, and in a very non-emotional way asked what was going on. I explained how I perceived her approach to me and how it was making her feel, and asked if I was doing something to cause this reaction. Imagine my surprise when she got very upset and apologetic. It turned out that a friend of hers had told her that I had wanted her position and was upset that I didn't get it. All this time she was worried that I was going to try and make her fail so I could take over her position! In the end she realized her friend was completely wrong. I didn't want her job, and, in fact, needed her to be successful so we could all be successful. To this day we are the best of friends!

- Our department head announced that the company was changing one of our key products, one that I had thought was always our best offering in the market. I was initially upset and was wondering if the company was going in a direction that I didn't agree with or wouldn't be able to feel passionate about. I scheduled a meeting with my supervisor to discuss it, and to my surprise he invited the department head as well. In this meeting I explained my perspective and confusion over the change, and wondered if he could provide more information so I could get my head around the new product. It turned out we were losing money on every single one of these that were sold. If we had continued on this path we could all have been unemployed within 3 months. Furthermore, the new product was modified based on feedback from our department and would result in a healthy profit. What a win-win situation! Our department contributed to launching a new product and I understood why the old one had to be discontinued. I felt so energized about the company and our management team after I left that meeting, and couldn't image having a better job anywhere!

Bad Responses

Never avoid this question by saying you haven't really had any conflict in your previous work experiences. This indicates that you're not being honest about situations, or are completely oblivious to events occurring around you, neither of which is good in terms of getting hired!

- I just keep my mouth shut, avoid conflict, and just do my job *[Note: We don't want employees to be "checked out". Someone who does this, or responds like this, wouldn't be a good candidate for most companies. We want active, engaged employees who are always looking to improve their roles, their teams, and the company].*

- I just avoid the person at work who seems to cause problems and treat me badly *[Note: We don't want employees that run away from conflict. What will be the next thing they run away from?]*

- I speak out in group meetings and express my disagreement when management introduces some new policy that is bad for us. They know when I'm upset.

Positioning possible negatives from your past

Never bring up an intense personal conflict with a co-worker or manager and "rant and rave" about how bad it got and "who did what". This will immediately show a lack of maturity, and possibly even expose anger concerns – either of which will give you a failing grade for the interview.

The trick here is coming up with a real example in your past that is based on a misunderstanding or inadequate information, and once real, honest communication occurred, the situation was resolved or transformed into a long term net benefit for you and the company. You need to demonstrate that everyone's perspective is normally valid based on what they know and their past experiences. Digging into that perspective and working through the differences is the key item we are looking for in your response.

Appendix: Career Fair Strategy

Let's talk about my direct experience both structuring and having my team run career fairs.

We've used 2 primary types over the years – "Open House" career fairs at the office, where we advertise and have hundreds of candidates show up and do on-site interviews, and then we participate in Career Fairs at hotels or convention centers where multiple companies are present.

Since Career Fairs at central locations are more common, let's talk about what is important when attending. My company approaches these as follows:

- We send one HR representative and 1 or 2 junior hiring managers to "man the booth".

- Their job is to assess job seekers who come to our booth interested in our company and our open positions.

- When they engage with candidates who stop by, they try and spend 5 to 10 minutes with each candidate.

- The outcome of this quick meeting is a mark on the resumes either to "follow-up with candidate for an onsite interview" or "pass on the candidate".

- We've also used a scoring system of 1-10, with 10 being "strong, bring in" and 1 being seen as "not a fit" (reject).

Now, as you can tell, this is intense. You have 10 minutes to impress either the HR rep or one of the hiring managers enough to get a call within 1 or 2 days to come in for an interview. So what do we look for? What interview questions and answers are important in this brief meeting to enable you to get selected for an interview?

Here are some key items that we use and train our representatives on for the career fair – if you understand and adhere to these you will dramatically increase your chances of getting the secret mark for a follow-up "real" interview in our offices:

1. Neat, professional appearance – either a suit or dressy business clothes. This shows us you're serious about a new position and you have respect for the time we're taking out of running the company to talk to you.

2. Some level of research done ahead of time. You should know what our company does, its key products and services, and ideally what functions exist in the local office [i.e. not all products/services may be provided out of each geographical office location].

3. We often have open positions posted on our company site ahead of time, so candidates who have reviewed these and know what openings exist and how they are a match for them have an excellent advantage.

4. Passion and energy – I cannot emphasize this enough. We will look at your resume for the basic qualifications, but the human interaction is key. We want to see energy and passion around our company and the business we're in. Low key individuals give across the impression of simply dropping resumes off at hundreds of booths in the hope that one will stick. This quickly gets your resume put into the "no follow-up" pile.

5. Of course a resume. Always have a steady stack of resumes with you. This is one forum where it makes a difference if your resume is printed on a nice heavy off-white card stock. Since we have to take these stacks back to the office and go through our notes, this document actually gets a lot of face time with managers ahead of getting a call.

a. This is a bit different than submitting a resume via email or mail for a position. In those situations the resume is scanned into our system by an administrative assistant and managers never see the original.

6. Ok – now this point is subtle – if we notice you're hitting every booth around us prior to coming to ours, this will reflect negatively. Again, it speaks to just doing a resume drop hoping for the best. Even if you want to talk to multiple companies around our booth, the best approach is to come to our booth from another area of the career fair, speak to us with passion and energy, and then walk out of sight to another part of the career fair. That looks to us as though you were solely interested in our opportunity, and works to your advantage, even if you come back to a nearby booth in an hour or two.

Keep in mind that we are looking, in a very quick review, for applicable experience on your resume. If we are hiring for a telephone based customer support position, we obviously look for a similar title or role on your resume in the initial scan. However, if you haven't had that exact role before, but have been in customer facing roles, be sure and highlight this experience during the brief 5 to 10 minute conversation and emphasize the importance of servicing customers.

For example: Let's say you're very technical but have only worked retail positions – GREAT! Emphasize your technical skills briefly, and then speak to how you were in a customer support position for your company and you feel you are good at understanding and addressing customer concerns to make sure they have positive experiences with the company and their products and services. This is a positive for this type of position, and if you do everything else above you will likely get selected for a follow-up interview at our offices!

One last note: Most of the time [but not always], we will not make any hiring decisions on the spot. This is a screening event to speak to hundreds of people and identify the 10 to 20 that we rank the highest to schedule "real" interviews. Some companies do hire on the spot, but in our experience these have been for high volume, high turnover positions, so just be cautious on that front [A good question to ask if they say they are hiring on the spot is to ask what their turnover rate is after 6 months!]

Appendix B: The Resume Game

Ever wondered where your resume goes after you submit it to a company? Almost all companies [especially larger ones] follow a very standard process from the time a resume is submitted, to the time you're sitting in the chair ready to ace the interview.

Understanding this process will help you perform your best at each step. Given there are thousands of applicants for every open position, you need to have every edge you can get to stand out from the crowd.

Click – you've submitted your resume to a company online.

Your resume is routed [often via a tool like Taleo, Oracle, and other HR business systems] automatically to the recruiting specialist assigned to the hiring manager. This role sits within the HR organization, and is often a specialized recruiting role versus a general HR resource. (At smaller companies it may be a more general HR individual or even the hiring manager who receives your resume.)

The recruiting specialist will often have multiple hiring managers and positions they are working with, and will scan (quickly read over in 2 to 3 minutes) incoming resumes roughly every 1 to 2 days for each open position.

I emphasize the word "scan" here. They don't have time to read cover letters, and these seldom if ever influence a decision to move a resume to the next step. I personally always advise against writing and submitting a cover letter. I think it is a waste of effort.

When they visually scan your resume [or in some cases rely on the HR software to do it automatically], they are looking for keywords that match criteria the hiring manager gave them. These keywords vary widely depending on what the open role is. My only advice here would be to include key terms and phrases in your resume that match the job description, assuming it is accurate relative to your skills and experience (Don't lie on your resume).

If a resume hits most of the required items from the hiring manager, it gets moved to a "screening" stack. The screening stacks are ones that have the potential to move on to the next step.

Often the specialist will send 4-8 resumes at a time to the hiring manager from the screening stack, seeking feedback on which ones to then schedule for a phone screen by the recruiting specialist. In some of my prior companies [and my current one] the recruiting specialist will actually make this decision himself based on his understanding of the type of candidate the manager is looking for.

Assuming your resume makes it to the phone screening pile, the next step will be for the specialist to contact you to schedule a phone interview.

Phone interviews typically last less than 30 minutes, and are used to ask a fairly specific list of questions developed in conjunction with the hiring manager. These will focus on specific skills, experience, and knowledge. However, the specialist is also assessing your energy levels, passion, and communication style on the phone. This is key, as often they will pass over candidates who have the hard skills needed but communicate poorly or come across as not interested. Do not be afraid to ask the person what his role in the organization is if he doesn't include that in his introduction to you. If it is a hiring manager you will want to treat this as more of an interview than a phone screening.

Assuming you come across as very interested, passionate, and potentially qualified for the position, the specialist will then move you to the "in person interview pile". (Out of town candidates may go through an additional phone screen with the hiring manager themselves.). Due to the always limited availability of the hiring managers and others on the interview team, the goal is to wait until 2 or 3 top candidates are ready and then to schedule them for interviews during the same week if possible.

At this point hopefully you have been scheduled for an interview. As you can see from the above, a couple of key items to keep in mind are:

- Ensure your resume has the right wording that will jump out at a recruiting specialist as a match for the position

- Treat the phone interview with importance. If you don't impress the recruiting specialist over the phone, the hiring manager will never know about you.

Afterword

I wrote this book because I have seen far too many qualified candidates self-destruct in interviews. This includes entry level as well as very senior candidates. Over the years I have read numerous books on how to interview well, and felt many of them completely missed the few key areas to focus on. Many of the existing books provide hundreds of questions and answers for you to read – some of which are good and many of which simply aren't important.

Furthermore, too many books and articles on interviewing were written by individuals that don't actually make the hiring decision. This includes human resource personnel, recruiters, consultants, head hunters, and many others that simply do not own the decision on whether a candidate will be hired. I strongly advise you to listen to managers that actually will make the hiring decision versus others involved in the process.

If this book has helped you, please feel free to provide a comment on Amazon that others may find helpful.

Best Regards, and good luck on your career journey.

Russell Tuckerton

Made in United States
Orlando, FL
19 September 2023

37089038R00028